Mindfulness

for people in a hurry

Ash

Book design by Ashley Bonetti
Buddha by Sudowoodo (*Shutterstock*)
Businessman by Robert F. Balazik (*Shutterstock*)
Tie-dye by P-Fotography (*Adobe Stock*)

ISBN: 9798751396473

To those who led the way,

thank you

Introduction

*"You don't have to be a monk to be mindful…
you just have to be present."*

———————————

Let's face it, mindfulness can be intimidating.

Between the obscure language and the unfamiliar concepts, we often find ourselves discouraged before we even begin.

The thing is, mindfulness should *simplify* our lives, not complicate them. There's nothing menacing about mindfulness. It shouldn't be a stressful, tiresome, or intimidating experience.

Mindfulness should be about one thing and one thing only: *being in the present.*

We spend so much of our lives on autopilot – never being where we are and never truly feeling anything.

If this is how our lives are spent, are we really living?

.   .   .

This book isn't magic. You won't be enlightened after one paragraph, or attain nirvana after a few pages; however, every day you will learn the tools to make your life a little bit better.

Every day you will learn how to show up to life – how to be present for each and every crazy, beautiful moment.

You will learn how to get your life back.

What you do with it is up to you.

Day 1-50

Day 1

*"You cannot take a future or a past breath. The
breath is always definitively in the present."*
— Rabie Hayek

Mindfulness is about being in *the now*. It's about
shifting your focus from what may have happened
in the past or what could happen in the future, and
instead focusing on the present moment.

You're here. You're alive. *Be here. Be alive.*

Soak it in. You'll never be in this moment again.

One Conscious Breath: In order to bring yourself
into this mindset, your mission today is to take one
conscious breath. At some point in your day, stop
what you're doing and breathe in deeply through
the nose, out through the mouth. Really focus on
that breath. Let everything else fade away. Allow it
to draw you back into the present moment. Allow
it to remind you that you're alive.

"You are under no obligation to be the same person you were five minutes ago."
— Alan Watts

When we practice mindfulness, our goal is learning to focus on each and every present moment. We leave the past in the past, and we don't worry ourselves with the future. We recognize that the only thing we'll ever actually experience is the present – this moment, here and now.

The problem arises when our ego enters the equation. We spend our lives creating this complex idea of who we are – what we like and dislike; what we can and cannot do. Then, we convince ourselves that we have to stay within these bounds. The thing is, *it's all an illusion*. You're a different person every minute of every day. The only thing standing between you and a new life is you.

Ideal Human: Make a list of the characteristics that an ideal person would possess. Are they generous? Loyal? Kind-hearted? Ask yourself what you can do here and now to be more like this person.

"When walking,
walk.
When eating,
eat."
−Zen Proverb

Food is our life source. It nourishes our bodies; it keeps us strong. But how often do we take it for granted? How often do we acknowledge where it comes from, or the journey it took to get to our plates? How often do we truly *taste* our food?

Mindful Eating: Eat your next meal mindfully. Truly taste your food. Chew each bite slowly and thoroughly, experiencing all of the flavors that your food has to offer. Somewhere in this process, take time to think about where your meal came from and how it will impact your body once you eat it. Take a moment to thank the earth for giving you sustenance for another day.

A vegan or vegetarian meal is suggested for this exercise.

Day 4

*"In every walk with nature one receives
far more than he seeks."*
—John Muir

When we hear the word *meditation*, we tend to visualize someone sitting on the floor in the lotus position, exhibiting perfect tranquility; however, meditation does not have to look like this.

We can have meditative experiences in lots of different ways – from walking to painting to gardening, to name a few. If what you're doing calms and focuses your mind, it is a kind of meditation.

Mindful Walking: Get outside and go for a walk; however, try not to bring any distractions with you. Shift your focus instead onto the walk itself.

Focus on your body, noticing the rhythm of your stride. How does walking make you feel?

Focus on your environment. What is happening around you? What do you see, hear, and smell?

"Acknowledging the good that you already have in your life is the foundation for all abundance."
−Eckhart Tolle

It can be easy to overlook the good moments in our lives, but we must realize that there are *so many* good moments. Why is it that we seem to notice the bad more than the good?

Well, research seems to suggest that we're wired this way. The ability to spot danger has been one of our most essential survival tools; however, nowadays we're hunted more by our thoughts than we are by any outside predator. It's crucial that we take the time to balance out the scales in our minds.

Gratitude Journal: Grab a notebook or even just a piece of scrap paper and write down everything that you're grateful for today. Did you wake up this morning in good health? Did someone hold the door for you, or smile at you on the sidewalk? Did you get to watch the sunrise? Learn to recognize and appreciate these moments.

---

*"Meditation is nothing but
taking a mental shower."*
—Yogi Bhajan

Most people, at least at first, have trouble learning how to properly meditate. One of the best ways to combat this is to try different types of meditation.

Shower meditation is probably the practice that parallels our everyday routine the most. In this exercise, we use our daily shower to guide us into a meditative state. It is a quick, easy, and effective way to learn the skills needed for meditation.

Shower Meditation: Turn to exercises for a short, guided shower meditation.

Day 7

*"The words you speak become
the house you live in."*
—Hafiz

Every word we speak is an opportunity, and on average, we speak about seven thousand words each day. This means that each day we are given seven thousand chances to brighten the world around us – seven thousand opportunities to make it a little bit better. How many of these words do we actually use for this purpose?

Our words shape the world around us. What kind of world do your words create?

Speak Positively: Before you speak today, let your words pass through three gates: *Is it true? Is it necessary? Is it kind?* Challenge yourself to follow these guidelines the best you can, and see how long you can last without straying from the path.

Day 8

*"When the breath wanders the mind also is
unsteady. But when the breath is calmed
the mind too will be still."*
—Svatmarama

They say eyes are the windows to the soul. If that's
the case, then breath is the front door.

Our breath changes dramatically based on how
we're feeling at any given moment. If we're in a
positive headspace, our breath remains deep and
slow; if we enter a more negative headspace, our
breath becomes shallow and rapid.

Breathing and feeling are *inextricably connected*
in our minds. This means that if we breathe in a way
our body recognizes as calm, it won't take long for
our minds to believe us.

Box Breathing: Close your eyes and take a deep
breath in through the nose for four counts, hold it
for four counts, and breathe it out through the
mouth for four counts. Allow your lungs to remain
empty for four counts, and repeat the process.

Day 9

*"If you don't become the ocean,
you'll be seasick every day."*
—Leonard Cohen

The earth is the one thing we're all connected to. It holds some of the greatest wonders; it contains some of the most breathtaking beauty. Yet, we try to disconnect from it. We build our houses, drive our cars, and wear our shoes. We do everything we can to put a barrier between us and nature.

The thing is, we *are* nature. The farther we get from the natural world, the farther we get from ourselves.

Grounding: Find a nice spot to kick off your shoes and give yourself back to nature. Make the choice to either go for a walk, stand and relax, or even complete some other task. Simply have at least ten minutes of uninterrupted contact with the earth.

Day 10

"Sleep is the best meditation."
— Dalai Lama

Nighttime is typically when our thoughts run wild. For most of us, it's the one time of day when we sit still long enough to get overpowered by our negative emotions. We question things we could have done better and overthink things we have no way of changing.

As is often the case, our thoughts do more harm than good in these situations. Our bodies need quality sleep, and we owe it to ourselves to work toward the calm frame of mind that allows this to happen.

By simply reserving a few moments to reflect and unwind before bed, we can set the stage for a clear mind and a peaceful night's sleep.

Sleep Meditation: Turn to exercises for a short, guided sleep meditation.

Day 11

*"No person has the power to have everything
they want, but it is in their power not to
want what they don't have."*
—Seneca

We all have preconceived ideas of what it takes to be happy. Whether it's wealth, success, or even love, we're always reaching for something that's just out of our grasp. We're always one step away from happiness, but we're never quite there.

There's a reason for this, and it's known as hedonic adaptation. Hedonic adaptation maintains that after any life event, either good or bad, we tend to return to our baseline level of happiness. We become accustomed to our new situation, and we find more things to want. And so, the cycle continues.

Negative Visualization: Reflect upon the absolute best things in your life. Then, picture your life without these things. Acknowledge the ways that your life would be different, and use this as a reminder to be grateful for the good that is already around you.

Day 12

"Lose your mind and come to your senses."
—Fritz Perls

Our senses are our ties to the present moment. While our thoughts may exist in any time or space, our senses are focused on what we're experiencing *right now*. There's no better way to center yourself than simply observing what's around you.

3-2-1 Senses: Find a quiet and comfortable spot, preferably outdoors. Take a moment to notice your senses. What do you see? What do you hear? What do you feel? Make a mental list of your experience and recite it aloud. Name three things you see, two things you hear, and one thing you feel. Repeat this process until you run out of sensations.

Day 13

"Close some doors today. Not because of pride, incapacity or arrogance, but simply because they lead you nowhere."
—Paulo Coelho

The world that surrounds us is ours to shape. And while we can't control every aspect of our lives, we can most certainly control where we place our attention. Make sure the things you give attention to are things that deserve to be in your world.

Nourish Your Mind: Get rid of the things that are dragging you down. Log off of social media. Turn off the news. Stop engaging with people who never have anything positive to say. Instead, try reading a work of classic literature. Listen to a song that lifts you up and makes you happy (try "Here Comes the Sun" by The Beatles). Surround yourself with people who inspire you to be better and make the world around you a better place to live.

Day 14

"We cannot hold a torch to light another's path without brightening our own."
—Ben Sweetland

Every little thing we do plays a part in shaping not only our world, but the worlds of everyone around us. From our actions to our words and our body language, we each do our part in creating the world we live in. What do you do to make this world a more positive place for us all?

Smile at Everyone: Challenge yourself to smile at each and every person you come into contact with today. Radiate genuine positivity. Put special effort into lighting everyone else's path, and in turn, you may also brighten your own.

Day 15

---

*"Within you, there is a stillness and a sanctuary
to which you can retreat at any time."*
—Hermann Hesse

If you had the power to go anywhere in the world, where would you go? Is your happy place the beach? Or the mountains? Maybe your happy place isn't a place at all, but a fond memory or a dream.

In any case, we all need somewhere we can go — a sanctuary we can carve out in our minds. Then, when the world around us feels unkind, we can spend some time exploring our own spaces. We can harness the power of meditation to truly *be* in these places. We can feel the sunshine on our skin at the beach or smell our favorite dessert baking in the oven of our childhood home. We can be where we want to be, when we want to be there.

Guided Imagery Meditation: Turn to exercises for a short, guided imagery meditation.

"There are only two ways to live your life. One is as though nothing is a miracle. The other is as though everything is a miracle."
— Albert Einstein

The chances of you existing are basically zero. You are the culmination of thousands of years of history – every minute that aligned perfectly to lead to this exact second. If even one moment in the entire history of the universe had happened differently, there's a good chance that you wouldn't have been born at all.

Your existence is, by all definitions, a miracle. Not only that, but your existence in *this* world is a miracle. What are the chances that you'd live in a world with electricity? With running water? What about a world where you aren't constantly being hunted? You could've been born at any time; or even still, you could've simply never been born at all.

Miraculous Perspective: Take a moment to reflect upon five miracles in your life. Write them down on a piece of paper and recite them back to yourself.

"You yourself, as much as anybody in the entire universe, deserve your love and affection."
—Author Unknown

We would *never* speak to another human being the way that we speak to ourselves – if we did, they would never talk to us again. Why should we treat ourselves any differently?

Positive Self-Talk: Make a list of your most valuable qualities. Focus less on physical appearance and more on inner characteristics. Would you consider yourself to be someone who helps others when they're in need? Are you someone who isn't afraid to stand up to others when you know that something is wrong? Write these attributes down on a piece of paper and read them aloud to yourself. Begin each line with "I am" (e.g. "I am kind" or "I am brave").

End your list with "I am worthy."

Day 18

*"The body is your temple. Keep it pure
and clean for the soul to reside in."*
—B.K.S. Iyengar

Our bodies are the vessels through which we experience the world. It can be easy to overlook the body's significance when we're trying to focus our attention inwards; however, we must remember to occasionally look outwards as well. We must learn to respect and care for our bodies the way that we do for our minds.

Deep Clean Your Body: Take some time today to truly care for your body. Begin by cleaning yourself thoroughly and intentionally. Exfoliate your skin and then moisturize it. Brush your teeth and don't skip out on flossing. Take note of any problem areas that may need your attention. If you can, dedicate some extra time to these areas (e.g. hydrate dry hair, open up clogged pores, etc.). Listen to your body when it tells you what it needs.

"If you want others to be happy, practice compassion. If you want to be happy, practice compassion."
—Dalai Lama

Compassion is one of the highest virtues in nearly every religion; however, while many groups find it fundamental, Mahayana Buddhists deem it essential.

Mahayana Buddhists believe that although one may achieve enlightenment or *nirvana* as an individual, true nirvana can only be attained through genuine compassion for others. We all must do our part to alleviate the suffering of others, and in turn, we'll be released from our own suffering.

Give Back: Take some time today and dedicate it toward helping somebody else. Consider looking into the process for volunteering somewhere in your area or reaching out to someone you know that's going through a tough time. Find a cause you believe in and commit to it.

Day 20

"Possession of material riches, without inner peace,
is like dying of thirst while bathing in a lake."
—Paramahansa Yogananda

One of the biggest threats to mindfulness is excess. And while excess in any regard is bad, an excess of material goods is perhaps the worst of all. These possessions distract us; they make us selfish. They clutter our worlds and our minds.

All of this isn't to say that we have to renounce *all* worldly possessions and become ascetic monks (unless we feel compelled to do so); however, it's absolutely still imperative to get rid of the things in our lives that we no longer need.

Give Away: Take some time to go through your belongings and determine which items you truly *need*. You'll probably find many things in your possession aren't positively contributing to your state of mind. Give these things away.

"Every person is a world to explore."
—Thich Nhat Hanh

Every person in this world knows something that you don't. Everyone has hopes and dreams, and experiences that are unique to them. Everyone has something worthwhile to teach and something worthwhile to say; however, it's often the case that we simply don't take the time to ask.

.

When we spend so much time isolated in our own thoughts, it can be hard to maintain empathy and understanding for others. We run the risk of getting stuck in an echo chamber of our own beliefs. We must take the time to interact authentically with others, both for the relationships themselves and for the sake of our character.

Explore Someone's World: Pick someone in your life and get to know the real them. Who are they? What do they dream about? What matters most to them? Dive in and give them your full attention.

Day 22

---

*"The soul becomes dyed with
the color of its thoughts."*
—Marcus Aurelius

A large part of our well-being lies not in our objective situation, but in our subjective experience of that situation. In other words, *the narrative that we tell ourselves about our circumstances is often more important than the circumstances themselves*.

If we visualize good things coming into our lives, we're more likely to feel as if we have these good things. On the other hand, if we constantly expect the worst out of every situation, we're likely to feel defeated regardless of the outcome.

We must learn to heed the color of our thoughts.

Our happiness, first and foremost, must come from within.

Visualization Meditation: Turn to exercises for a short, guided visualization meditation.

Day 23

"Don't judge each day by the harvest you reap, but by the seeds that you plant."
—Robert Louis Stevenson

Every day we plant metaphorical seeds. Minute by minute and seed by seed, we lay the groundwork for who we're going to be. Are you setting yourself up to be a flower or a weed?

Do you like the seeds that you're planting?

Plant a Metaphorical Seed: Consider a goal that you've set for yourself and think of something small you can do *today* to make it more attainable. Set aside ten or fifteen minutes to plant this seed for your future self.

"All the flowers of all the tomorrows
are in the seeds of today."
—Indian Proverb

While we're waiting for our metaphorical seeds to take root, it's also good practice to plant physical seeds. There's no better way to connect to nature than to watch it grow before our very eyes.

The ability to give life to something is probably the closest thing to magic that we can experience as humans. We become part of a cycle that's larger than ourselves, and in learning to cultivate these seeds, we learn to cultivate patience, virtue, and love.

Plant a Physical Seed: Find a seed and plant it. Care for it, and watch it grow. Feel the intense joy when you see the very first sprout pop up out of the dirt. Recognize that it grows and blooms just as you do. Recognize that *you created life where there was once only dirt*. By planting that seed, you changed your little corner of the world.

Day 25

"Unexpressed emotions will never die. They are buried alive and will come forth later in uglier ways."
—Sigmund Freud

There's a common misconception that mindfulness allows us to conquer our emotions; however, our feelings aren't enemies that must be battled or mountains that must be trekked.

Our feelings are just that — *feelings*. They're temporary states of mind that arise out of our existing circumstances. Sometimes they're good and sometimes they're bad, but in either case, we must allow them to run their course.

Emotional Expression: The next time you experience a strong emotional response to something, allow yourself to thoroughly feel it. Express this emotion in any way you need to (nonviolently, of course). Then, when you're ready, acknowledge the impermanence of this emotion. Repeat this phrase:

"I'm feeling _____ right now, but it won't last forever."

Day 26

"Everything that irritates us about others can lead us to an understanding of ourselves."
—Carl Jung

A large step in learning how to let go of our negative emotions lies in understanding *why* we feel the way that we do. Do we dislike the people around us because they're truly that awful, or is there a simpler explanation? Is it possible that we're jealous of them in some ways? Or that we lack some kind of understanding about them?

Oftentimes we project our own negative emotions onto others; however, we must learn to treat our attitude toward others as a mirror through which we can see ourselves. It may be the case that the traits we despise in others are really just characteristics we hate within ourselves.

Don't Bother: The next time that you encounter someone who irritates you, stop and consider *why* you're irritated. What does it say about you?

"To understand everything is
to forgive everything."
—Leo Tolstoy

Human beings are capable of doing so much good, but they're also equally as able to cause so much harm. When someone directs that harm toward us, it can be hard to overlook their behavior; however, we must remind ourselves that no action self-originates. Whatever harm has been done to us has been the buildup of countless moments in this person's life — a life that we've never lived. We'll never fully understand how this person came to be who they are, and while this doesn't excuse what they've done to us, it does offer a new perspective.

We may not forgive the action, but we must forgive the person.

Forgiveness Meditation: Turn to exercises for a short, guided meditation on forgiveness.

---

*"Forgive yourself for not knowing what you
didn't know before you learned it."*
—Maya Angelou

Sometimes the hardest person for us to forgive is ourselves; however, we must learn how to do this. We couldn't have known back then what we know now, even if it feels that way in hindsight.

Our personal failures seem so harsh because they're just that – *personal*; however, there isn't a human being in the world that has never made a mistake. We must remember that a life spent reliving our mistakes opens the door for a life spent *repeating* our mistakes. We can't go back and change what we did in the past, but we can stop allowing it to define our future.

Self-Forgiveness Meditation: Turn to exercises for a short, guided meditation on self-forgiveness.

---

*"I'm not afraid of storms, for I'm
learning how to sail my ship."*
–Louisa May Alcott

It can be hard to calm the seas when it feels as if waves keep crashing onto shore; however, if we learn to control the wind, we can learn to manage the current.

The way that we breathe affects every part of our bodies – from our lungs to our heart and our nervous system. By understanding how to harness this energy, we can begin to regulate our body's response to negative emotions.

By learning how to lull the waves, we can still the seas.

4-7-8 Breathing: Whenever you feel your heart rate start to increase today, take a moment to breathe in through the nose for four counts, hold it for seven counts, and breathe out through the mouth for eight counts. Repeat this process three to four times, and you should notice your heart rate steadily decreasing until you're back to baseline.

"A day without laughter is a day wasted."
−Charlie Chaplin

They say that laughter is the best medicine, and in many ways, this is true. Laughter can relieve stress, improve our mood, and relax our bodies. Studies show that it can even reduce anxiety and boost our immune systems.

Nevertheless, as we get older, we get told that we need to be more serious. We laugh less and stress more. How can we expect to be happy in a world with so little laughter?

Laugh Therapy: Make yourself laugh today. Not just a chuckle − *a full laugh*. Keep it going for at least a few minutes.

If you're unable to coax out a natural laugh, it's okay − just laugh anyway! It's been shown that fake laughter can have all of the same benefits as real laughter.

Day 31

"Yoga is the journey of the self,
through the self,
to the self."
−Bhagavad Gita

The word *yoga* comes from the Sanskrit root *yuj*, which means "to unite." In yogic practice, we aim to unite both our bodies with our minds and our personal reality with the collective reality that surrounds us.

The yoga that most of us are familiar with is known as hatha yoga. This yoga is distinguished by its focus on the physical form. Hatha yoga can help us become more in tune with our bodies, and it can provide us with a comfortable space to exist in the present moment.

Hatha Yoga: Turn to exercises for a short, guided introduction to hatha yoga.

*"If speaking kindly to plants helps them
grow, imagine what speaking
kindly to humans can do."*
—Author Unknown

Compassion is an essential virtue that must be cultivated daily; however, we may not always have time to organize grand gestures expressing our goodwill. Instead, we should also focus on individual, small practices we can implement each day to help us become more compassionate.

One simple act, such as the giving of a kind word, can have a rippling effect on the rest of the world.

One Kind Word: Take the time to brighten someone else's day today. Whether it's a stranger on the street or an old friend, give a genuine compliment to someone. Try not to comment on temporary characteristics such as looks, but to instead focus on more essential qualities.

Day 33

"If your compassion does not include yourself, it is incomplete."
—Jack Kornfield

We can appear to be the most compassionate people in the world; however, if we don't also love ourselves, then we're not truly compassionate. We must work toward self-love the same way we work toward loving all of those around us.

Self-Compassion Meditation: Turn to exercises for a short, guided meditation on self-compassion.

*"Morning is when I am awake and
there is a dawn in me."*
—Henry David Thoreau

Of all the hours in a day, those that surround the sunrise are perhaps the most beautiful. There is a certain sense of quiet and tranquility that exists only during these hours, and those who linger in bed may never get the chance to experience it.

Rise and Shine: Set an alarm for fifteen minutes before the sun is set to rise. When the alarm goes off, get out of bed and head outside (or to a calming spot that has a view of the sky). Make yourself comfortable and simply *be*. Bask in the feeling of nothingness. There's nothing you need to do and nowhere you need to be. The world around you hasn't started yet – it's just you and the sunrise. Take it in while you can.

If you're already an early riser, go ahead and set an alarm to wake up fifteen minutes earlier than usual. You can use this time to center yourself and set your intentions for the day.

*"Music is indeed the mediator between
the spiritual and the sensual life."*
—Ludwig van Beethoven

Music is one of the few pastimes that human beings can get truly lost in. When we immerse ourselves in it, we become connected to the entire universe — we become the bird singing in a tree and the child humming a tune halfway across the world. We break down our barriers and merge into one unified spirit.

There's something divine about music. We don't have to question or analyze it — we can *feel* it. How many things in life can you simply feel?

Get a Rhythm: Get a small group together (if you can) and try your hand at a drum circle. Use drums if you have them, and if you don't, use whatever is nearby that will make a sound. Play by yourself if no one else is around. Get a rhythm going and *feel* the music. Don't play perfectly — just play immersively.

"I am haunted by the need to dance. It is the purest expression of every emotion, earthly and spiritual. It is happiness."
—Anna Pavlova

Like music, dance relies on *feeling*.

When we dance, our movements exist entirely as a reaction; as such, any amount of outside thought is a direct threat to our performance. We must shift our attention instead to feel the world around us. *We must exist solely in the present moment*.

Feel the Rhythm: Put on some music and just *dance*. It doesn't matter how you look. Turn off your mind and let the rhythm guide you.

*"It is very rare or almost impossible that an event
can be negative from all points of view."*
—Dalai Lama

The Chinese philosophy of Taoism teaches us that darkness and light (*yin & yang*) aren't the opposites of one another, but rather the complements of each other. They're two coexisting forces that depend upon one another to survive. Without the existence of darkness, there'd be no way of knowing what it means to experience light. Conversely, if we'd never encountered light, we'd have no way of knowing when we're in darkness.

Yin and yang also teaches us that no situation is absolute. In every yin, there's some amount of yang; in every yang, there's some yin. This means that in even the darkest situations, there's always a little bit of light to be found.

Find the Yang: Recall a time when it felt as if you were in total darkness, and identify the light that came out of it.

*"It is better to light a candle than
to curse the darkness."*
—Chinese Proverb

We tend to think of meditation in terms of absence — absence of thought, absence of emotion, etc.; however, we must learn to think of it instead as *presence*. Presence of consciousness; presence of focus. Presence of serenity and acceptance. Presence of presence itself.

One type of meditation, called trataka meditation, brings this particular idea to life. In this exercise, participants choose something small (such as the flame of a candle) and focus their attention entirely on this one object. They allow everything else to fade into the background, and they achieve clarity through their concentration. They light a candle instead of cursing the darkness.

Trataka Meditation: Turn to exercises for a short, guided trataka meditation.

Day 39

"So divinely is the world organized that every one of us, in our place and time, is in balance with everything else."
—Johann Wolfgang von Goethe

We constantly strive to find balance in the world around us; however, it's also essential that we discover a sense of balance *within* us. Alternate nostril breathing, or *nadi shodhana* in Sanskrit, is designed to accomplish exactly this.

In this exercise, every breath we take is directed toward a specific part of our bodies. The breaths we take through our left nostrils aim to stimulate the right side of our brains (the side known for emotions and creativity), while the breaths we take through our right nostrils aim to stimulate the left side of our brains (the side known for analysis and logical thinking).

Alternate Nostril Breathing: Turn to exercises for a short, guided introduction to ANB.

"When you feel the suffering of every living thing in your own heart, that is consciousness."
—Bhagavad Gita

Karma is often misdefined as cosmic punishment — a supernatural law and order system where what goes around comes around; in reality, karma is *action*. If we cultivate good action (compassion, empathy, generosity), we get to live in a world with these characteristics; however, if we foster negative action (indifference, apathy, greed), that's the world we're left to live in.

Which world would you like to be a part of? What can you do to get there?

Conscious Diet: Acknowledge that all living beings are the same — all want to live and be free from suffering. Do your part to further this vision of the world by trying out a vegan or vegetarian diet for the rest of this book. Then, as you eat each meal, take a moment to reflect on how choosing nonviolence makes you feel.

"No one does wrong willingly."
—Socrates

This one's tricky, because at any given moment, people certainly *can* do wrong willingly. We know that it's wrong to lie; however, we often do it anyway. We know that violence is unwarranted; however, we commit acts of cruelty all the same. We weigh the pros and cons of our actions, and we *purposely choose* whether or not we want to do something.

All of this is true; however, we must realize that these statements aren't mutually exclusive. We can choose to do the wrong thing, but still be making this choice because we think that it's right.

Our evil derives from ignorance, not from intention.

Gain Perspective: Place yourself in the shoes of someone you disagree with and take a moment to contemplate their choices. Why might they feel that they made the best possible decisions under the circumstances they were given?

Day 42

*"Chanting opens the heart and
makes love flow within us."*
—Swami Muktananda

One of the biggest struggles we encounter in meditation is the dilemma of the wandering mind — the idea that the harder we try not to think about anything, the more intensely we begin to think about everything.

When our thoughts inevitably start to run wild, it helps to have some sort of anchor in place to bring us back to center. Chanting is one of the best anchors we have available to us. Whenever we feel our mind begin to wander, we simply repeat our mantra until the intrusive thoughts fade away.

Mantra Meditation: Choose a mantra (a word or a few words that hold immense significance to you) and use it to perform a ten-minute meditation. If you don't have a mantra, use Om.

Day 43

*"It took me four years to paint like Raphael,
but a lifetime to paint like a child."*
−Pablo Picasso

If you ask a child to draw you a picture, they'll usually do so with no further instruction. You don't have to describe what you want the picture to look like or how you want it to be drawn – you simply sit back and watch as they sketch out whatever they're feeling *in that exact moment*.

As these children turn into adults, things become more complicated. They begin to scrutinize every line of every picture they draw – that is, if they even draw at all. They focus less on the *experience* of the art and more on the aesthetic of it. They lose the inner child and gain an inner critic.

Mindful Painting: Turn to exercises for a short, guided introduction to mindful painting.

"Act without doing;
Work without effort."
—Laozi

Taoists such as Laozi believe there's an underlying natural order within the universe. They refer to this order as the Tao (i.e. "the way" or "the path"). Whenever we live our lives in accordance with this order, we're said to be in harmony with the Tao.

The Tao often reveals itself through *wu wei*. Wu wei, which can be translated to "non-doing" or "non-action," exists as a state of being in which we act in complete accordance with the natural order of the world. In this state, our actions are so intuitive that they simply flow out of us — we don't have to force them or think deeply about them. We act without acting, and we do without doing.

Experience Wu Wei: Immerse yourself in an activity that makes you feel as if your actions are effortless. Get a good flow going and give in to the Tao.

Day 45

*"The quieter you become,
the more you can hear."*
—Ram Dass

Language has been the key to our survival for thousands of years. It's helped us learn and thrive, and pass the knowledge of how to do so onto the next generations. It's been perhaps the greatest advancement in the history of mankind. But how much language is too much?

Over time, the act of speaking has become less about communicating ideas and more about filling space. We've become uncomfortable with silence and unable to simply observe the world around us.

We must learn to be okay with simply observing. We must learn to embrace the silence once again.

Day of Silence: Give your voice a rest for the day. Be silent as much as possible (or entirely silent if you're able). Focus on taking in the world around you without worrying about how you'll respond to it.

*"The bamboo that bends is stronger
than the oak that resists."*
—Japanese Proverb

Life isn't meant to be strict and structured – *it's
meant to have flow*.

Our existence on this earth is unpredictable, and
everything that we know can change at any given
moment. It's our job to figure out how to find
harmony in the chaos. From our minds to our
bodies, we must learn to bend before we break.

Tai Chi: Turn to exercises for a short, guided
introduction to Tai Chi.

Day 47

*"Set your life on fire. Seek those
who fan your flames."*
—Rumi

The Sanskrit word for breath (*prana*) refers to more than just respiration – it's more accurately translated to mean "life force" or "vital energy."

Hindus believe that every breath we take is a spiritual experience. Every inhale contains a spark of the universe's energy and every exhale allows it to flow through our bodies. Prana is the key to life; it's energy in its purest form.

In a time of darkness, prana can set our lives ablaze.

Breath of Fire: Sit up straight with one hand on your stomach. Take a full breath in through your nose, feeling your stomach expand as you go. Then, quickly and forcefully push this breath back out through your nose, feeling your stomach depress. Repeat this process for thirty seconds, inhaling gently and exhaling vigorously.

"I could put my thumb up to a window and completely hide the Earth. I thought, 'Everything I've ever known is behind my thumb.'"
—Jim Lovell

Sometimes our problems seem catastrophic. When this is the case, we have to give ourselves a little bit of perspective. How much do these problems really matter in the grand scheme of things?

The View from Above Meditation: Turn to exercises for a short, guided meditation on perspective.

"We shape clay into a pot, but it is the emptiness inside that holds whatever we want."
—Laozi

If you asked a Mahayana Buddhist to describe you, they would probably call you empty.

Emptiness, or *sunyata* in Sanskrit, is the idea that everything is connected – that everything that exists, exists interdependently.

There is no *you* that's separate from the world around you; instead, you're an amalgamation of *everything* – from the trees and the sea to the sun and the moon. You're one expression of existence in an immense and limitless universe.

You're nothing, and that makes you everything.

Emptiness: Reflect upon the way in which you're empty. Write down five things that you're full of (e.g. the paper you write on is full of the sun and soil that helped it grow as a tree, the lumberjack who chopped it down, the miller who refined it, etc.).

Day 50

Q: *"How are we to treat others?"*
A: *"There are no others."*
—Ramana Maharshi

Close your eyes. Take a deep breath and picture the ocean. Watch the motion of the waves as they rise and fall. Allow them to crash into shore and slowly drag themselves back.

Notice how each wave is a little bit different from the other. Some waves are bigger than others, some move faster than others; but ultimately, they're all part of the same ocean.

Without the other waves, and without the movement of the ocean as a whole, they wouldn't exist at all.

The waves are us. We're the ocean.

In the end, we're all one.

Circle of Hierocles Meditation: Turn to exercises for a short, guided meditation on connectedness.

Exercises

Shower Meditation

Turn on the water and find a nice, comfortable temperature for yourself.

Step into the shower, taking a few deep breaths as you go.

Feel the water as it flows down your body.

Visualize all of your worries being washed away by the power of the water.

Allow all fear, doubt, and insecurity to slowly be cleansed from your body.

Wash these feelings down the drain and allow your negative thoughts to be carried down with them.

You are clean. You are new.

You are ready to face anything.

Sleep Meditation

Turn off the lights and put away any distractions.

Get into bed and lie flat on your back. Feel yourself sink into the mattress.

Take a deep breath in and out. Release the weight of the day.

Starting with your feet, relax your body parts one by one – feet to legs, legs to abdomen, abdomen to chest, and so on – until your whole body has relaxed.

Turn your attention onto your breath. Take a deep breath in – inhaling the fresh, calm air around you.

Let that same breath out, allowing your exhale to carry any stress or negativity that you may be harboring along with it. Repeat this several times.

It is time to acknowledge that your day has come to an end. You have nowhere else to be in this moment. You have nothing else to do. This is only a time to rest and be still.

Allow your breath to slowly guide you to sleep.

Guided Imagery Meditation

Find a quiet, comfortable spot and close your eyes.

Release any tension that is in your body.

Draw in a few deep breaths – in, out...in, out.

When you feel ready, start to picture yourself in your happy place. Remember that this can be anywhere you want it to be. It may be an actual place, a memory, or even a fantasy that you have created.

Once you have found your place, begin to *really* picture it. How does the air feel in this place? What colors do you see? What can you smell?

Allow yourself to envision every single detail.

Then, when you feel that you have fully arrived in your place, allow yourself to truly relax. You have made it. The rest of the world cannot bother you here; there's nowhere else you need to be. You are safe and you are free.

Stay here as long as you need.

Visualization Meditation

Find a quiet, comfortable spot for yourself.

Take a moment to contemplate the feelings that you want to manifest.

Assign these emotions to a color that's meaningful to you (e.g. yellow for happiness, light blue for serenity, etc.).

Assign a different color to the feelings you want to rid yourself of (e.g. dark blue for sadness, black for stress, etc.).

Once you're able to clearly picture these colors, close your eyes and redirect focus onto your breath.

Envision the color you've chosen to incorporate into your psyche. Consider everything that this color represents for you.

Visualize this color filling up your body. Every breath you take allows more of it to enter your lungs, spreading the energy from your head down to your toes.

At the same time, envision the color you've chosen to rid yourself of. Consider everything that this color represents for you.

Visualize this color being pushed out of your body with every exhale. Every breath you take carries more of it out, cleansing and purifying you in the process.

Repeat this process until you feel satisfied with your progress.

Forgiveness Meditation

Find a comfortable position and close your eyes.

Shift your focus onto your breath. Feel the air as it gently flows into and out of your body.

Maintain this focus for a few moments. Then, when you're ready, give your mind permission to wander.

Allow yourself to recall the way others have harmed you in the past.

Create a safe space for these thoughts to enter into your awareness, but do not allow any of them to linger for more than a moment. Simply watch them as they come and go.

Notice how these thoughts make you feel.

Do you feel anger? Disappointment? Sadness?

Do you feel wronged?

Acknowledge these feelings and allow yourself to feel them one last time.

Then, with a deep breath, let them go.

It is time to acknowledge that you can't keep carrying this anger around with you. It's not good for anyone, and especially not for yourself.

Understand that you may never fully know *why* these things happened. Although you were able to feel the effects, you didn't personally endure the causes. You'll never know if you would've done differently after walking in this person's shoes.

Visualize this person in your mind, and then repeat these words: _____ *is human. He/she makes mistakes. There have been times in my life when I've made mistakes, and in those times, I needed forgiveness. I can do the same for* _____.

Then, when you're ready, forgive this person. Say aloud, "I forgive you, _____. I forgive you."

Repeat this process as many times as you need.

Self-Forgiveness Meditation

Sit somewhere comfortable and close your eyes.

Feel your breath as it slowly moves your body up and down. Focus on this sensation for a moment.

As you maintain focus on your breath, go ahead and give your mind permission to wander.

Allow any grievances that you hold against yourself to enter into your awareness.

Let these thoughts pass through your perception, but don't allow yourself to fixate on them. Simply watch them as they come and go.

Focus for a second on how these thoughts make you feel.

Do you feel guilt? Anger? Remorse?

Do you feel fear?

Acknowledge these feelings and allow yourself to feel them one last time.

Then, with a deep breath, let them go.

It is time to acknowledge what you already know — that you're worthy of forgiveness.

You can't change the past; however, you can pick up the pieces that you've broken and use them to build a new, stronger foundation for the future. You can let your mistakes teach you how to be better.

Repeat these words: *I am human. I make mistakes. It's all a part of my journey. I can't change what has already happened, but I can relieve myself from carrying this great burden. The only thing that's in my power is to be better now.*

When you're ready, forgive yourself. Say, "I forgive you, _____."

Breathe in, breathe out, and repeat these words.

Breathe in, breathe out, repeat.

Hatha Yoga

Balasana
Child's Pose

Marjaryasana
Cat

Gomukhasana
Cow

*Adho Mukha
Svanasana*
Downward Dog

Uttanasana
Standing
Forward Fold

Anuvittasana
Standing
Backbend

Tadasana
Mountain

Virabhadrasana II
Warrior II

Trikonasana
Triangle

Uttanasana
Standing
Forward Fold

Kumbhakasana
Plank

Bhujangasana
Cobra

Kapotasana
Pigeon

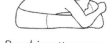

Paschimottanasana
Seated
Forward Fold

Savasana
Corpse

Hold each pose for 3-4 breaths

Self-Compassion Meditation

Find somewhere quiet and comfortable to sit.

Take a few deep breaths and close your eyes.

Notice the sensation of your breath as your chest rises and falls. Focus on this feeling for a moment.

Then, when you're ready, complete a brief body scan. Take note of any areas where you feel pain or tension. Try your best to soothe and relax these areas.

Once your body is relaxed, turn your focus toward your mind. Ask yourself: *What do I need to hear right now?*

Whatever this message may be, send it to yourself in this moment.

Repeat these words: *May I be kind to myself. May I accept myself. May I be happy. May I have peace.*

Breathe in, breathe out, and repeat these words.

Breathe in, breathe out, repeat.

Trataka Meditation

Find a quiet area and sit in a comfortable position.

Dim the lights.

Place a candle at eye level a few feet away.

Light the candle and focus all of your attention on the flame.

Watch the flame as it flickers and moves.

Steady your breathing – deep breaths in through the nose and out through the mouth.

Allow yourself to acknowledge any other thoughts that may pop up during this time, but do not allow these thoughts to linger. Always turn your focus back to the flame.

Continue this exercise for ten minutes.

When the time is up, allow your eyes to rest for a moment while you reflect on your experience.

Alternate Nostril Breathing

Close your eyes and raise your right hand toward your face.

Press your thumb down onto your right nostril and draw in a deep breath.

As you finish inhaling, press your ring finger onto your left nostril until both sides of your nose are closed.

Hold this position for a moment, then release your thumb and exhale from your right nostril.

With your ring finger still covering your left nostril, inhale now from your right nostril.

At the end of your inhale, hold both nostrils closed for a moment.

Exhale from the left nostril.

Repeat this cycle six times.

Mindful Painting

Gather any painting supplies that are available to you. If you don't have any available, you can use markers, colored pencils, crayons, etc. – anything that'll make a mark.

Take a moment to clear your mind, breathing in a few deep breaths. Remind yourself that there's no right or wrong way to be creative. The end result isn't important. All that matters is the process – the *now*.

If you wish, you can draw a few lines and use these as a starting point; however, it's important to note that we're not trying to create any particular sort of image. *Don't direct your lines toward anything.* Simply allow your arm to flow around the canvas.

Paint your canvas. Allow your thoughts to fade into the background as you go.

Take each brushstroke as it comes. When you *feel* like using the color yellow, use the color yellow. When you *feel* that a spot needs a splash of blue, use some blue. *Remember that there's no set plan.*

Continue this process until you feel finished.

Tai Chi

Tai Chi is less about specific movements and more about *how* you move.

Your feet should be rooted to the ground with your knees slightly bent.

Your movements should be slow and fluid.

Your breath should be calm and controlled.

You're opening up channels of energy, and in your movements, you're shifting this energy around.

You want to make a way for the energy to flow *through* you.

Repeat this movement cycle 4-5 times

The View from Above Meditation

Find a comfortable position and close your eyes.

Turn your focus onto your breath for a moment – feel your chest as it slowly rises and falls.

Picture yourself now from an outside perspective. Visualize looking down and seeing yourself exactly as you are in this moment.

As you keep your eyes focused on your body, you can slowly begin to *zoom out*.

Zoom out until you are able to see your entire neighborhood. See people going about their days – getting ready for work, visiting loved ones, etc.

Zoom out again until you can see your whole county. Notice everyone (including yourself) getting smaller and smaller as your view expands.

Zoom out until you can see your whole region; your whole state; your whole country. Realize that you and everyone you have ever known are now merely dots on a map.

Zoom out again until you can see the entire planet. As you are watching, billions of little specks are moving around the earth, feeling as if their problems are huge; however, these people and their problems are no longer visible from up here.

Zoom out until you can see the whole solar system; the whole galaxy; the whole universe. The earth is now merely a speck in the darkness, and you are just a speck on that speck. Gaze upon the universe for a moment and appreciate its vastness.

Now, begin to zoom back in.

Zoom in to our galaxy; our solar system; our planet.

Zoom in to your country; your state; your region.

Zoom in to your county; your neighborhood; and then finally, zoom back in on you.

Shift back to your normal perspective and open your eyes when you feel ready.

Circle of Hierocles Meditation

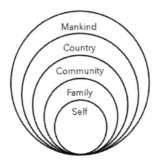

Find somewhere quiet and close your eyes.

Draw in a few deep breaths – in, out...in, out.

Now, envision your connection with others as a series of concentric circles.

In the center circle, you have yourself.

In the second circle, you have your family.

In the third circle, you have the people in your community.

In the fourth circle, you have everyone in the country.

In the fifth and final circle, you have all of mankind.

As you sit and visualize these circles, your aim is to pull each one closer to the center.

Begin by visualizing a bright light surrounding you. This light represents your love and affection.

At first, the light only encapsulates you. It fills you with warmth and comfort.

Slowly envision this light expanding to include your family, both biological and figurative. Where they were once pushed away, now they are part of you.

Expand your light once again to include the people in your community – the ones that surround you every day. Glow until these individuals become part of your family.

Expand your light until everyone in your country can feel its warmth. Welcome these people as you would your own neighbor.

Expand your light once more until all of mankind is illuminated. Every member of the human race can feel your light – they're all included in your affection.

Maintain this feeling for a moment.

When you're ready, open your eyes.

Afterword

Memento mori.

If you take anything away from this book, this is perhaps the most important thing. Translated into English, this phrase comes out to *"remember you will die."*

While that may seem morbid, it's important to acknowledge that our time on this earth is limited. We can't do everything there is to do; we can't see everything there is to see. We must use our time *wisely*.

We don't have forever, but we most certainly have right now. *We have to make it count.* Take the trip you've been dreaming about. Tell someone special how much you care about them. Look inwards and better yourself. One day you'll wish you had the chance to do these things, but it'll be too late.

For now, it's not too late. Do the things you want to do. Be the person you want to be.

And, perhaps more than anything, **be here now.**

What is a good life? How do we get there?

Ash has spent her life chasing the answer to these questions. From scouring centuries-old texts on dusty bookshelves to receiving formal education in psychology, philosophy, mindfulness, and religion, it's clear that she has never given up the pursuit.

And while it may forever remain a pursuit, and the journey may never end, Ash intends to share her findings every step of the way.

Made in the USA
Middletown, DE
18 November 2022

15466055R00085